DO WHAT YOU LIKE

JOBS IF YOU LIKE
Writing

Stuart A. Kallen

San Diego, CA

About the Author

Stuart A. Kallen is the author of more than 350 nonfiction books for children and young adults. He has written on topics ranging from the theory of relativity to the art of electronic dance music. Kallen won a Green Earth Book Award from the Nature Generation environmental organization for his book *Trashing the Planet: Examining the Global Garbage Glut*. In his spare time he is a singer, songwriter, and guitarist in San Diego.

© 2025 ReferencePoint Press, Inc.
Printed in the United States

For more information, contact:
ReferencePoint Press, Inc.
PO Box 27779
San Diego, CA 92198
www.ReferencePointPress.com

ALL RIGHTS RESERVED.
No part of this work covered by the copyright hereon may be reproduced or used in any form or by any means—graphic, electronic, or mechanical, including photocopying, recording, taping, web distribution, or information storage retrieval systems—without the written permission of the publisher.

Picture Credits:
Cover: SeventyFour/Shutterstock
10: fizkes/Shutterstock
19: PeopleImages-Yuri A/Shutterstock
34: fizkes/Shutterstock
50: fizkes/Shutterstock

LIBRARY OF CONGRESS CATALOGING-IN-PUBLICATION DATA

Names: Kallen, Stuart A., 1955- author.
Title: Jobs if you like writing / by Stuart A. Kallen.
Description: San Diego, CA : ReferencePoint Press, 2025. | Series: Do what you like | Includes bibliographical references and index.
Identifiers: LCCN 2024036196 (print) | LCCN 2024036197 (ebook) | ISBN 9781678209889 (library binding) | ISBN 9781678209896 (ebook)
Subjects: LCSH: Authorship--Vocational guidance--Juvenile literature. | Mass media--Vocational guidance--Juvenile literature. | Communication--Vocational guidance--Juvenile literature.
Classification: LCC PN153 .K34 2025 (print) | LCC PN153 (ebook) | DDC 808.02023--dc23/eng/20240814
LC record available at https://lccn.loc.gov/2024036196
LC ebook record available at https://lccn.loc.gov/2024036197

Contents

Introduction: For the Love of Words	4
Content Marketing Manager	7
Public Relations Specialist	15
Editor	23
Scriptwriter	31
Technical Writer	39
Grant Writer	47
Source Notes	55
Interview with a Grant Writer	58
Other Jobs If You Like Writing	61
Index	62

Introduction:
For the Love of Words

Some people think of writing as a chore, something that must be done to accomplish a task. Others love words and enjoy the act of writing. They relish stringing sentences together, whether they are writing blogs, social media posts, movie reviews, podcasts, novels, or any of the other genres that revolve around the written word.

Many aspire to write a blockbuster script or best-selling book, and those goals are attainable for the few who have spent considerable time practicing those crafts. For many, though, the best place to acquire and hone writing skills is online. You can start a blog and express your opinions on whatever subject captivates your interest. As you establish an online presence, you can promote your blog with a steady stream of tweets, status updates, and email blasts.

Some young adults are earning money writing social media posts for major brands. They are reviewing toys, bands, video games, TV shows, and movies. Others are writing comedy pieces and sports roundups or blogging about travel, fashion, and beauty. Writing and editing gigs are available to kids as young as thirteen on the website Fiverr, while others are earning money on the blogger platform Medium. Magazines such as *Literary Orphans* and *Cricket* also hire young writers. Although most of these gigs do not pay much, they provide excellent experience that can lead to a career.

Fill a Niche, Find Your Voice

Writers who thrive focus on niches they can fill. Rather than trying to appeal to everyone, these writers focus on creating a very specific type of content that their customers are eager to buy. And the freelance writing and editing market is made up of numerous niches that fit almost every style, taste, and skill level. For example, if you have a flair for entertainment, you might search for work writing speeches, jokes, podcasts, and video scripts. Budding entrepreneurs might find success in the field of business-to-business (B2B) communications. Writers in this line of work produce ad copy, corporate blogs, grant applications, product descriptions, and reports called white papers that cover complex business-related issues. Fiction lovers can take jobs in creative writing, ghost writing, and script writing. Those who enjoy helping others might take gigs writing personal correspondences, résumés, and cover letters.

There is little doubt that artificial intelligence programs like ChatGPT are taking over some of the online writing tasks once performed by writers. But experts say even the most advanced AI programs do not compare to human writing skills. Content created by AI programs can be error-ridden, biased, or filled with nonsensical sentences referred to as AI hallucinations. As tech policy writer Julia Angwin says about AI, "In my eyes, it's looking less like an all-powerful being and more like a bad intern whose work is so unreliable that it's often easier to do the task yourself."[1]

There is another key difference between a living writer and an advanced computer software program. The human touch provides a unique creative style known as the writer's "voice." Screenwriter John Lopez explains the concept of voice: "Writing is communication. Writing is connection. A writer makes their thoughts echo in another's head. Whether it's poetry, ad copy, or emails to your mom, good writing resonates with its audience."[2]

Artificial intelligence cannot generate resonating content that contains a high level of creativity, precision, and originality. But developing your own distinctive voice requires commitment to the art of writing. This means reading anything and everything that will help you develop your talents, from popular novels to ad copy and even technical manuals. And of course, a writer must write. Freelancer Zawn Villines explains, "I've made a very good living as a writer. It is both harder and easier than you think. Harder because making a career as a writer requires exceptional organization and productivity. Easier because once you establish yourself, success requires only that you sit down each and every day to write."[3]

The Bureau of Labor Statistics says the job outlook for writers and authors is expected to grow by 4 percent through 2032. This is about as fast as the average for all jobs. While some entry-level jobs, such as B2B writing, might be disappearing due to AI, there is still a demand for skilled writers who can express their original ideas in their own voice. Lopez attests, "As we all find ourselves drowning in cheap, hollow, GPT-generated [trash], actual human connection might prove more valuable than ever."[4]

Content Marketing Manager

What Does a Content Marketing Manager Do?

The internet is a visual medium filled with photos, videos, and pop-up windows to attract attention. But the online world would not exist without millions of words uploaded by freelance writers every day. Well-written blogs, infographics, listicles, memes, email blasts, and press releases are central to what is known as content marketing. Those who work as content marketing managers write engaging content that is aimed at attracting clicks, likes, and shares from a targeted audience. The content is designed to help businesses and individuals define a brand, product, or service while attracting customers and boosting sales. As content marketing manager Hayley Folk describes the job, "Anytime you see or hear about my company—either in the blog, website, or emails in our public-facing persona—the [content] marketing team is involved. The marketing team owns the presentation of the company and how it appears from things like the logo, the website, the overall messaging and our social platforms like Twitter [X] or LinkedIn."[5]

Producing the most effective marketing content requires managers to understand search engine optimization (SEO). The SEO process

A Few Facts

Typical Earnings
$73,954 in 2024

Educational Requirements
Bachelor's degree in marketing, communications, writing, or digital media

Personal Qualities
Analytical, creative, good communicator

Work Settings
Full time in offices

Future Outlook
Growth of 6 percent through 2032

evolved with search engines like Google and Bing. These platforms use artificial intelligence (AI) algorithms that search for key words in blogs, articles, and other content. When users enter words in search boxes, the algorithms present the content with the closest keyword matches at the top of the page. This higher search engine placement helps drive internet traffic to the top sites.

The SEO process involves generating blog posts that are five hundred to seven hundred words long. These articles often contain multiple paragraphs on a specific content topic, and they repeat the same keywords that users search for. Content marketing managers face the challenge of creating posts that are helpful and readable yet still stuffed with relevant keywords to drive traffic to the site. But the SEO process is very important, according to a 2020 study by *Search Engine Journal*. Websites in the number one position on a search engine results page have a 25 percent click-through rate, meaning one-quarter of users click on the link. The click-through rate drops to 15 percent for position two and down to 2.5 percent for position ten.

Content marketing managers combine their knowledge of SEO with AI programs. Predictive AI allows marketing managers to better understand user engagement and shares. This allows content managers to move beyond keywords and fine-tune their work to achieve better results for their clients. Digital advertising expert Gabriel Lumagui explains the importance of AI in content marketing: "AI is not just a tool; it's a partner. Its capabilities can elevate content marketing to heights previously unimagined."[6]

A Typical Workday

Content marketing managers work with clients to plan, develop, and implement strategies that drive customers to a website or physical store. This is often done by making a three-part plan called a sales funnel or marketing funnel. The purpose of the on-

Research Is Essential

"Blindly churning out generic content will not offer much to an effective digital marketing campaign, which is why research is such an essential part of the process. Not only is research required for background on each piece of content, but it's also necessary to study the fundamental elements of [content] marketing. A regular part of the job is reading about effective keyword strategies, getting to know SEO updates, and learning about user experience—which is what brings content to life. Without this knowledge, there wouldn't be much intention with each piece of content, creating a disorganized and ineffective campaign."

—Marissa Storrs, content marketer

Marissa Storrs, "'So What Do You Do for a Living?' A Day in the Life of a Content Marketer," Pennington Creative, 2024. www.penningtoncreative.com.

line marketing funnel is described by content marketing manager Alexa Collins: "Marketing funnels represent the journey of [an online] customer from 'hi' to 'buy.'"[7] The "hi," or greeting stage, is known as top of the funnel, or TOFU. Content at the top of the funnel is meant to attract the widest audience possible and retain their interest for an extended period. The content generally consists of blogs and how-to articles based on a customer's business. Content marketing managers who write these posts often spend time reading industry publications and tech articles related to the subject matter.

Middle-of-the-funnel (MOFU) content is aimed at those who already know the brand and are interested in seeing more information. Content marketing managers working on MOFU content write scripts for short videos. They gather interesting facts and figures that can be used to make eye-catching graphs and charts. And marketing managers use specialized software to

The process of writing engaging blogs, listicles, email blasts, and other promotional materials requires content marketing managers to meet with clients. Together they develop strategies for driving customers to the client's business.

write and produce webinars. The goal is to encourage customers to engage further by downloading case studies, e-books, and in-depth research reports called white papers.

Content described as bottom of the funnel (BOFU) is made up of live demos, product trials, and customer references. These items are meant to convert casual shoppers into buying customers. Content manager Casey Crane explains, "BOFU is where it's at. It's about taking all of those sales qualified leads (people who know what they want or need) and guiding them to purchase your products."[8]

After building a sales funnel, a content marketing manager will plan an editorial calendar that lays out how, when, and where the content will be rolled out. Content marketing managers hire freelance writers, video producers, and others and oversee their work. One content marketing manager known as cfwang1337 says most of the day is spent writing blog posts, but editing work written by others is time well spent. "Editing stuff other people write is a huge multiplier," says cfwang1337. "Not everyone writes particularly well, but almost everyone knows something you don't, and you can always clean up someone else's writing and save yourself some original research."[9]

Those who manage marketing content creation set style guidelines for a project and ensure work is progressing on schedule and completed on time. They sketch diagrams that can be used by graphic designers to create artwork and websites. And like almost all workers, content marketing managers spend time attending meetings, sending and receiving texts and emails, and collaborating on the phone.

Education and Training

Job listings for content marketing managers usually require candidates to have a bachelor's degree in marketing, communications, writing, or digital media. Those who do not have an undergraduate degree can improve their employment prospects by completing one of the numerous affordable online courses and university programs that focus on digital marketing strategies. For example, Arizona State University and Oregon State University both offer online courses for those who want to earn a bachelor of arts in mass communications and media studies at a reasonable price.

Skills and Personality

Content marketing managers need to have a passion for reading and writing. In addition to spinning out interesting and engaging blogs, emails, and other content, the job requires workers to stay up-to-date on the latest advances in digital communications. This means reading articles, studies, and research papers on complex topics such as keyword strategies, artificial intelligence, and SEO.

Content marketing managers also need to be tech savvy to develop websites, navigate the internet, and use social media platforms to achieve the best results. They must use tools and software that allow them analyze website data, click-through rates, and other social media engagement metrics such as time spent on a web page and leads generated. This requires content marketing managers to understand Google Analytics, the Hootsuite social media management platform, content management system software, project management software such as Asana and Trello, and SEO tools like Semrush. Content developer Justin Paulsen explains the importance of data and analytics. "Online marketplaces often speak to huge numbers of prospective customers at once," he says. "This means that measuring the efficacy of a given piece of content will require the ability to play with numbers and data to discern patterns and trends. In short, the content marketer must also be comfortable with statistics."[10]

Leadership skills are also important for content marketing managers because many manage teams. Good leaders can communicate clearly and persuasively, in writing and in person. This is useful when running meetings, managing people of various skill levels, and diplomatically explaining technical issues to customers, managers, and executives.

Working Conditions

Content marketing managers are mid-level professionals who generally work full time in the marketing department of an employer's office. The job can be stressful when deadlines approach and might require working more than forty hours a week.

Employers and Earnings

Content marketing managers typically work for companies that specialize in advertising, public relations, and digital communications. Around one-quarter are self-employed, according to the Bureau of Labor Statistics (BLS).

New Adventures Every Day

"I need to be highly organized to pull off the number of projects we have on the go. I rely on my old-fashioned handwritten to-do list as well as a project management tool, Jira, to allocate and manage tasks and deadlines. . . . Every day is different (which I love). Proofreading and subediting blogs and articles, briefing the team to produce an eBook, meeting with an employment law expert to deliver a webinar—these are just some of the activities in my day. . . . Producing content is a team effort—the entire marketing team works together [and] I feel so lucky to work with such a wonderful group of talented people."

—Annette Micallef, content marketing manager

Quoted in HAO, "A Day in the Life: Content Marketer," Balance the Grind, April 14, 2021. www.balancethegrind.co.

The career ladder for content marketing managers has several steps. The entry-level position, called content specialist, involves creating and publishing digital content. Content specialists were paid around $60,000 annually in 2024, according to the employment website Indeed. Those with three to five years of professional experience can move on to become content marketing managers, who earn a median annual income of $73,954 a year. Some managers become content strategists, who focus solely on analytical research, marketing engagement, and long-term planning. They can earn around $78,377 a year. The highest-paid content marketers can move up to an executive role, earning more than $175,000 annually as a vice president of digital marketing or chief marketing officer.

Future Outlook

Most companies could not thrive in the digital environment without content marketing managers. The BLS says the career field is expected to grow by 6 percent through 2032, which is slightly faster than the average for all occupations.

Find Out More

American Association of Advertising Agencies (4A's)
www.aaaa.org
Known as the 4A's, this organization provides comprehensive information about advertising and business development. The Learning Institute section on its website offers workshops, certification, leadership training, and educational courses.

American Marketing Association (AMA)
www.ama.org
The AMA provides education and certification for future marketers and professionals already working in the field. Its website offers members guidebooks and academic journals, a job board, educational videos, and webinars.

Content Marketing Institute
https://contentmarketinginstitute.com
The website for this content marketing training institute provides free educational material for prospective content marketing managers, including blogs, white papers, webinars, and research insights.

Public Relations Specialist

What Does a Public Relations Specialist Do?

There are countless rock bands trying to make it in the entertainment business, and Amanda Cagan is there to help them succeed. Cagan works as a public relations (PR) specialist, or publicist. As the name implies, public relations specialists create publicity for their clients. Cagan has worked with many successful rock bands over the years, including Green Day, Korn, Styx, and Maroon 5. She promotes them by writing press releases and speeches. Like most PR specialists, Cagan uses social media to publicize her clients, posting related videos and photos and then monitoring the postings to ensure that they are effective and reaching her targeted audiences. She also responds to comments and questions from the public.

With more than a dozen well-known clients, Cagan is very busy. She often hires other writing professionals, such as skilled biographers, to lighten her workload. "I rely on the bio writer to nail those ideas that will give me the story points that will make the band more interesting to media," she says. "I may have a great idea of what the band is but a good writer makes it take on a whole life."[11]

Public relations specialists like Cagan focus on the entertainment

A Few Facts

Typical Earnings
$66,750 in 2023

Educational Requirements
Bachelor's degree

Personal Qualities
Good communicator, self-motivated

Work Settings
In an office 40 to 60 hours a week, including nights and weekends, with some travel

Future Outlook
Growth of 6 percent through 2032

Build Your Brand

"Use your social media including Facebook, Instagram, TikTok, and Twitter to create an online presence while simultaneously developing skills that will serve you in your PR career. . . . Evaluate what posts and hashtags get you more engagement in the form of likes, followers and comments and integrate your findings into future posts. Engage with influencers, editors, stylists, and bloggers in an organic way on these platforms. . . . Your own blog is a great way to further differentiate yourself while interviewing for PR jobs. You'll learn what elements make a successful blog post/story and can use that knowledge when drafting press releases, pitches, and invites."

—Lindsey Smolan, public relations agent

Lindsey Smolan, "4 Easy Ways to Gain PR Experience (When You Don't Have Any)," PR Couture, 2023. www.prcouture.com.

industry, while others work for corporations, organizations, and individuals, including business leaders, bloggers, and influencers. Public relations specialists referred to as press secretaries perform similar work for politicians, government agencies, and administrators. Whatever their title or their client base, public relations specialists are skilled at communicating with the public and media sources, including journalists, publishers, and radio and television producers. A public relations specialist who goes by the handle toppragenc explains the importance of the job: "Public Relations [specialists] play a vital role in helping businesses build and maintain a positive image, enhance their reputation, and communicate effectively with their target audience."[12]

A Typical Workday

The job of public relations specialist is often described as both difficult and fun. Coordinating media campaigns with powerful, successful clients can be exciting. And promoting their interests in a compelling, creative manner can be satisfying. But working in public relations can be challenging, too. Public relations specialists are often required to organize several promotional events, product launches, and press conferences in a single week. This requires them to attend several meetings a day while managing events through numerous phone calls, texts, and emails. The job involves coordinating interview schedules, responding to inquiries, and lining up teams of people from camera operators to caterers. Deidre Gaskin, publicist for the Harlem Globetrotters basketball team, describes her typical day:

> I usually have a bunch of emails to check, pitches to create and/or follow up on, maybe some materials I need to write or create such as a press release, media alert, bios, press kits, copy for marketing materials including website, social media, or emails. On more hectic days, I can be organizing a community event, wrangling up media to cover it, executing a press conference or back-to-back calls with clients for interviews and team meetings in between.[13]

Some public relations specialists take on the additional task of holding workshops to help their clients understand the importance of developing good PR strategies. Workshops also provide training that allows clients to sharpen their speaking skills so they can effectively communicate with the press and the public themselves.

Education and Training

A college degree is not necessary for those who have previous PR experience. Cagan, for example, grew up in a show business family. Her father was a Hollywood composer, and her aunt is a Grammy Award–winning songwriter. After high school Cagan went to work as an assistant for her aunt's publicist.

Those who do not have family connections should seek a bachelor's degree in public relations, communications, writing, or business. Gaskin offers this advice to those who are curious about the PR business: "Take the time to learn the industry, learn whatever niche you want to serve in and just be great in all aspects of PR. Be a great writer, be a great communicator, be a great researcher, be a great person. I say intern and volunteer as much as you can, that way you can build your resume and build your career."[14] Gaskin adds that internships can be extremely helpful when seeking employment after graduation. Interns at PR agencies attend events and help develop marketing campaigns and brand awareness initiatives.

Those who focus on volunteering can make their own opportunities. Volunteers build up their résumés by offering to promote local businesses, charities, or social media influencers. Prospective PR specialists can also work to build their own brand on social media by writing blogs and submitting articles to websites that are focused on public relations topics.

Certification is not necessary for public relations specialists, but being certified enhances your credibility and opens doors to new employment opportunities. There are numerous publicist certifications, including Accreditation in Public Relations, Strategic Communication Management Professional, Hootsuite Social Marketing Certification, Digital Marketing Certification, and Google Analytics Individual Qualification. All accreditation is offered to students and professionals through online courses.

Skills and Personality

Public relations specialists are strong writers who use proper grammar and spelling to create a constant flow of blogs, press releases, and other materials. And it helps to be a multitasker who can work fast. Cagan says one of her most important qualities is her ability to move around a keyboard at lightning speed. "I'm

Some public relations specialists conduct workshops to help their clients understand the importance of developing good PR strategies.

proud to say that [I am] a fast typer," she asserts. "I work better on my wireless keyboard that I know like the back of my hand. I'm constantly opening and closing files, moving emails around in my in box, making changes to press releases and reports, doing research online, posting client clips on my socials, and typing up interview options and schedules, so all the typing has to be done quickly!"[15]

In addition to their other talents, PR specialists need to have soft skills. At the most basic level, soft skills might be thought of as manners. They include patience, politeness, and speaking clearly and concisely. Other soft skills include the ability to plan, organize, and pay attention to details. And it helps to have a sense of humor and learn to take criticism with grace.

You Need to Be Organized

"There are so many people involved [when publicizing a movie] . . . helping the press get everything that they need to run their coverage. If they have an interview request for a specific talent, we have to gather all the information and take it to the talent's personal publicist to coordinate with their schedule. Then we have to go back to the press, with what day and time work. We make sure they have screened the film or the project, that they have photos with the proper credits. . . . It's also putting out fires and jumping in to problem-solving mode."

—Breanna Hogan, publicist for Netflix

Quoted in Carol Ann Underwood, "The Life of a Publicist," Plank Center, 2021. www.plankcenter.ua.edu.

It is important to understand and develop soft skills before taking a job, as the experience of PR specialist grluser571 illustrates: "I speak as someone who initially started out in [a public relations] agency environment who had to learn all of this the very hard way and believe me when I tell you it was not pleasant. I'm grateful for what it taught me despite how hard it was to even have to learn the ropes of the industry in such a way."[16]

Self-motivation is another required soft skill for PR specialists. Those who can look ahead, analyze situations, and take care of issues before they become major problems have a better chance of success. A PR specialist called TechPRIsLife says, "Every day will be filled with last-minute requests, urgent projects and a lot of information to take in. Find solutions that help you identify how to get everything done in priority order."[17]

Despite the demanding schedule, publicists are expected to be quick-witted and responsive in high-pressure situations. This requires a strong focus on the work-life balance to avoid burnout.

Working Conditions

Clients of public relations specialists rarely follow a nine-to-five workday schedule; most public relations specialists work more than forty hours a week. Events are often scheduled at night or on weekends and might involve travel across town or across the country. Public relations specialists who work with touring musical acts and celebrities on promotional tours might be required to travel extensively.

Employers and Earnings

Public relations specialists often begin their careers as junior publicists in entry-level jobs at PR agencies or ad agencies. They might move up to become publicity coordinators or communications associates. Mid-level job titles include communications manager, media relations specialists, and brand publicist. Senior publicists work as directors of public relations, directors of communications strategies, and vice presidents of brand communications. Some publicists who have gained experience at agencies launch their own businesses or are self-employed.

The Bureau of Labor Statistics says the median annual salary for a public relations specialist was $66,750 in 2023. Those who worked in government as press secretaries earned an average of $76,140, while those employed at advertising agencies could expect an annual income of $74,250.

Future Outlook

Individuals, businesses, and organizations understand the need to promote themselves effectively on all types of media. This means the job outlook for public relations specialists is projected to grow faster than the average for all occupations, at 6 percent through 2032. Those who can expertly navigate the ever-changing social media landscape will be in high demand in the foreseeable future.

Find Out More

Hootsuite Academy
https://education.hootsuite.com

Hootsuite is one of the most popular social media management platforms. Hootsuite Academy offers a wide range of industry-recognized certifications, such as Social Marketing Certification and Advanced Social Media Strategy Certification.

International Association of Business Communicators (IABC)
www.iabc.com

The IABC provides career advice, certification, and webinars to business communication professionals. The association offers a student membership program that provides global resources, industry connections, and learning opportunities.

Public Relations Student Society of America (PRSSA)
www.prsa.org/prssa

The PRSSA is the student-based chapter of the Public Relations Society of America, which has more than four hundred chapters throughout the world. The organization specializes in professional development but also offers scholarships and awards and provides information about internships and jobs.

Editor

What Does an Editor Do?

Most readers are familiar with the horror stories of Stephen King. Since 1974 King has written 65 novels, which have sold over 400 million copies worldwide. While King is widely acknowledged as an immensely talented writer, he is not the only one who perfects his books before publication. As King says, "The editor is always right. . . . Put another way, to write is human, to edit divine."[18]

As King notes, writing for publication is common. According to industry statistics, 500,000 to 1 million titles are published in the United States every year. Countless other professionally written works, including newspaper and magazine articles, are also published. And it is safe to say that most of these pieces have been carefully read by one or more editors.

There are several different job titles for editors. Most who are just beginning their careers work as copy editors. These professionals read articles and manuscripts, checking closely to ensure there are no spelling, grammar, or punctuation errors. At newspapers and magazines, copy editors also write headlines and make sure articles are fair and factual. Many copy editors are freelancers who work on a variety of projects, including

A Few Facts

Typical Earnings
$75,020 in 2023

Educational Requirements
Bachelor's degree

Personal Qualities
Good reading skills, detail oriented, creative

Work Settings
Indoor in offices, 40 hours a week with overtime

Future Outlook
Freelance work likely to increase as traditional jobs decline

novels, scripts, blogs, scientific papers, and even résumés and emails.

Developmental editors mostly work in the book publishing industry. These editors focus on aspects of plot and character development in novels and other works. Developmental editor Megan Close Zavala writes, "Developmental editing focuses on 'big picture' things like [story] structure and content and theme. Basically, I read through a manuscript and . . . make changes and suggestions directly on the document, as well as [writing] questions in the margins."[19]

Those who are referred to as acquisition editors or executive editors specialize in evaluating manuscripts and articles from writers. Acquisition editors understand consumer and marketing trends and seek books and other written content that will generate profits for the publisher.

These job titles can be fluid. At large publishing companies, an editor might specialize in a specific niche. Freelancers or individual editors at smaller publishers might perform all these different tasks themselves.

A Typical Workday

The daily lives of editors depends on where they work. Those who are employed by publishers typically begin their workdays sifting through emails from authors and colleagues and query letters and book proposals from prospective authors. Editors who are not self-employed attend a lot of meetings. They might pitch proposals to their publisher for books they want to acquire or discuss sales of previously published books. Editors meet with authors to hammer out contracts, go over changes to manuscripts, or determine whether deadlines are being met.

Russell Davis performs many different editing tasks for a book publisher in Maine. Davis says he works from 9:00 a.m. until 6:00 p.m. and sometimes stays late. And most of that time

The Importance of Reading

"One of the most important things to remember about working as a freelance editor is that in order to do your job well, you should read—a lot! Reading not only sharpens your mind and hones your skills for spelling, grammar, and syntax, it also keeps you up-to-date on the competition out there faced by your clients who are writers. Knowing this competition and knowing what publishers are publishing enables you to provide informed, solid advice when your client requests comprehensive feedback from you."

—Tonya Thompson, freelance editor

Tonya Thompson, "A Day in the Life of a Freelance Writer," Servicescape, December 27, 2019. www.servicescape.com.

is not spent reading and editing books. Davis says during the course of a day, "I'll receive (on average) more than 100 e-mails, and get between 15 and 25 phone calls. I'll review production proofs, answer correspondence from writers, draft editorial letters. I may write cover or catalog copy, work with an artist on the cover art, a designer on the cover design, and negotiate a book contract. I rarely read at the office, especially full manuscripts. Usually, I read at home, a few hours on a week night, quite a bit more on the weekend."[20]

Like Davis, self-employed editors spend many hours a day on tasks that are not related to reading and correcting manuscripts. Freelancers need to promote their work on social media, maintain their portfolios on gig websites, respond to inquiries from potential clients, and keep new projects coming in. As freelance editor Tonya Thompson explains, "If you haven't sought out new work and additional clients, you'll find yourself to be out of work. This is the dreaded 'feast or famine' that many freelance editors experience and it can be challenging to avoid unless you're working daily to attract new business."[21]

Education and Training

Some editors develop a love for reading, writing, and language at an early age. This might lead them to focus on English courses in high school. In these classes students read literature while honing their writing, spelling, and grammar skills. Prospective editors can gain experience working on their high school newspapers and, later, college newspapers.

Most employers require editors to have a bachelor's degree in English or a related field such as communications or journalism. This educational requirement is necessary for freelancers seeking editing gigs on websites such as Scribbr and Scribendi. Because editors must possess specific knowledge of grammar, punctuation, and other language skills, editing gig platforms want freelancers to submit résumés or other proof of experience. Scribendi requires editors to have an undergraduate degree and at least three years of experience editing, writing, or teaching language. The experience requirements are not too strict. For example, writing for a school newspaper or unpaid tutoring count as experience on Scribendi. Once the site accepts a résumé, freelancers are required to pass an editing test; they are given a document with many errors that need to be corrected.

Some publishers offer student internship positions for those seeking hands-on experience. In addition to copyediting tasks, interns read and evaluate submissions, respond to queries, prepare manuscripts for publication, and sit in on meetings.

Editors who want to improve their career prospects can earn certification through a few different educational institutions, including New York University, UC San Diego Extended Studies, and the University of Chicago. The American Copy Editors Society offers the Poynter ACES Introductory Certificate in Editing, a three-level program that is considered the industry standard for communications professionals.

Skills and Personality

Editors need to be detail oriented to pick out errors in spelling, punctuation, and continuity, or consistency of characters, plot, and places throughout a book. A strong appreciation of the written word is helpful, according to freelancer editor Heather Mitchell. She writes, "Like most people in the editorial field, I've always loved books. I still fondly remember the first book I read, *A Fly Went By*, sitting on my mother's lap before I started kindergarten. Even as a busy high schooler, I always had a book that I was reading."[22] Those who read a lot develop good communication skills. They can use their writing skills to clearly explain changes and corrections to authors.

Good editors need to draw on creative skills when coming up with story ideas, writing headlines, and rewriting paragraphs of manuscripts. Having an interest in a wide range of topics is important for editors who might work in different genres that might include nonfiction, historical romance, or science fiction.

Working Conditions

Editors work full time in offices, homes, and remote locations. They are likely to work overtime when deadlines loom. The job can be stressful at times since editors are expected to deliver content that is error free.

Employers and Earnings

Some editors are employed full time by publishing companies, newspapers, and magazines. Others work for educational institutions and scientific and technical firms. The Bureau of Labor Statistics (BLS)

The Value of Time Management

"I only have a limited amount of time to work in peace and quiet, so I make the hours count. I prioritize my projects by deadline, but if there are no rushes I'll focus chunks of time on each project so I never feel like I'm behind on anything.

"Typically I'll start by proofreading or editing a blog post or article for a client, which I skim through first so I get a grasp of the subject and tone. I keep a notebook nearby so I can jot down any notes or issues that I want to research later or make sure I address."

—Phon Baillie, freelance proofreader and editor

Phon Baillie, "A Day in the Life of a Work-at-Home Proofreader and Editor," Edit Republic, 2024. https://editrepublic.com.

says around 12 percent of editors are self-employed, but the number might be higher. Government statistics are not as reliable when it comes to counting the self-employed.

In 2023 the median annual pay for all editors was $75,020. This figure was a little lower than the average for digital editors employed by content providers and social networks. Those who worked in the entertainment industry were the highest earners, bringing in $104,720, according to the BLS. Editors in the newspaper business were lower on the pay scale, earning an average of $56,900. The BLS says the lowest-earning editors made $39,790, while the highest-paid 10 percent earned more than $138,290.

Future Outlook

The BLS says the demand for editors is expected to decline by 4 percent through 2032 as the traditional print media sector continues to shrink. Tonya Thompson explains, "Magazines and other publications have been hit hard in recent years by a readership that increasingly consumes its news and information online or via smartphones. The financial strength of many publications has weakened and is showing signs that it will continue to do so."[23] However, Thompson notes that she has benefited from these changes because more publications are turning to freelance editors instead of maintaining an in-house staff. And despite the declining employment figures, the BLS says about 11,600 new job openings for editors are projected each year through 2032.

Self-employed editors who build good résumés can use their experience to move on to other writing gigs. Freelance editor Stephanie Leguichard says:

> While I would ideally like to be paid to write full-time, for me writing hasn't been as lucrative or reliable as editing. . . . [Editing] can vastly improve one's writing skills—it's a great way to sharpen one's grammar, tone, and style and to develop a keen sense of how to make one's writing flow as well as possible. In my time as an editor, I've become much more adept at improving sentence structure and paragraph structure in my own writing.[24]

Find Out More

American Copy Editors Society (ACES)
https://aceseditors.org
Members of ACES include editing professionals, teachers, and students. The ACES Academy offers scholarships, editing courses via webcasts, and editing certification through the Poynter Institute.

American Society of Magazine Editors (ASME)

www.asme.media

The ASME is the trade organization for professional editors of magazines and websites. The society provides student scholarships, an internship program, a senior mentor program, and a job board.

Scribbr

www.scribbr.com

This editing and proofreading platform attracts students who need help with academic papers and other assignments. Prospective editors can search the website's knowledge base to find information about language rules, artificial intelligence tools, definitions, and citing sources.

Scriptwriter

What Does a Scriptwriter Do?

There is an old saying in Hollywood; hundreds of people work on a film, but one person gets all the credit. That one person is usually a famous director or a superstar actor. But blockbuster movies and hit TV shows would not exist without creative people known as scriptwriters or screenwriters. Screenwriter Geoffrey D. Calhoun explains:

> Screenwriting is the art and science of crafting stories for film and television. Screenwriters are the architects of stories, laying the foundation upon which every other aspect of filmmaking is built. Without a script, directors have no vision to bring to life [and] actors have no characters to embody. . . . The screenwriter's role is to create the blueprint for the entire production, turning ideas into dialogue, scenes, and sequences that tell a compelling story.[25]

Most stories are made up of three acts, which provides a basic format for scriptwriters to follow. In the first act, viewers meet the main

---

A Few Facts

Typical Earnings
$38,000 to $100,006 in 2023

Educational Requirements
None, but a bachelor of arts in screenwriting or filmmaking is helpful

Personal Qualities
Good communication skills, persistence, patience

Work Settings
Home office

Future Outlook
Increase of 4 percent through 2032*

*This number applies to all writers

characters and are introduced to their individual situations. In the second act, the main characters are confronted with a problem that seems unsolvable. In a typical third act, the problem is resolved. Once a plot is divided into three acts, a scriptwriter creates individual units of action called scenes. Each scene is defined by a time and place, such as *interior—suburban home-kitchen-night*. In every scene, a scriptwriter describes details of the setting, which in a thriller might include important objects, such as a knife on the table. Scenes also describe actions and emotions expressed by actors and dialogue that is spoken.

In addition to creating production blueprints for TV and feature-length films, scriptwriters create scripts for short films, television shows, podcasts, web series, and stage plays. Some write TV and radio commercials and scripts for computer games.

A Typical Workday

Scriptwriting is a creative art, and scriptwriters rarely have typical working days or hours. Successful screenwriter Ron Osborn, whose credits include the film *Meet Joe Black* and the television series *The West Wing*, says, "If this is the first day of a new script, I have decided it's so because I've spent a number of days/weeks/months/years ruminating on the idea, throwing various brain droppings written on napkins, scraps of paper, yellow legal pad pages, into an ever-growing folder."[26]

Like most screenwriters, Osborn first develops a summary or logline for a story. Loglines are used to sell, or pitch, a story to producers in a meeting, and they commonly can be conveyed in about a minute. Some loglines might be just a few words that summarize the story, such as "Ant-Man versus the Wasp." After settling on a logline, a scriptwriter creates a treatment, a slightly longer document that describes the main characters and provides a short synopsis of the story. Content writer Luke Leighfield writes, "Your synopsis should give a good picture of your story,

> ### Write a Script, Then Another and Another
>
> "That first screenplay that you write, burn it. It's not ready. . . . Write the second one. Maybe then you kinda find the voice a little bit. Put that one aside. The third one you write, you're gonna learn a lot from the first two you've written. . . . [If you] realize something that you're writing in the third screenplay would work in the first, steal from yourself. Go back to that first screenplay and then hone that one. Re-write it. . . . Maybe burning it is an overreaction. That first screenplay that you wrote becomes your first spec."
>
> —Ryan Saul, literary manager
>
> Quoted in Lee Jessup, "Screenwriting," Lee Jessup Career Coaching, January 4, 2021. www.leejessup.com.

including the important 'beats' (events) and plot twists. It should also introduce your characters and the general vibe of the story. Anyone who reads it (hopefully a hotshot producer) should learn enough that they start to feel a connection with your characters, and want to see what happens to them."[27]

After the various elements come together, most scriptwriters will create a script using industry standard software such as Final Draft or less expensive alternatives like Celtx or WriterDuet. These programs format scripts so that one script page is equal to about one minute of screen time. This means that an average script for a ninety-minute movie is about ninety pages long.

Writing scripts can be difficult. While an experienced scriptwriter might create a script in a few weeks or months, some production blueprints can take years. And writing is only a small part of a scriptwriter's job. Scriptwriters spend most of their time trying to sell scripts that are completed. This means writing query letters, making phone calls, and sending emails and texts to line up meetings with talent agents, producers, and studio heads.

Like most writing, scriptwriting tends to be a solitary activity once the writer is ready to put his or her ideas down on the page. Scriptwriters often spend a lot of time just thinking about different ideas and approaches.

Education and Training

Many colleges offer bachelor's degrees in screenwriting, filmmaking, and other aspects of the film industry. Courses provide immersive experiences for students who learn how to write, direct, and shoot films while earning a degree.

A college degree is helpful but not necessary to pursue a career in scriptwriting. However, it takes a lot of reading to be a great writer, and scriptwriting is no different. Those who want to master the art need to read as many scripts as they can. This is easily done; there are hundreds of scripts from every era and genre available online for free at SimplyScripts or the Writers Guild Foundation. Prospective scriptwriters can pick a movie they like and read the script while watching the film.

How-to books are also helpful for budding scriptwriters. There are dozens available online and at libraries and bookstores. Scriptwriter Ken Miyamoto describes his learning process: "I didn't go to film school. My education was in the Film & TV aisle at [the bookstore] Barnes and Noble. I read every single screenwriting book I could find. I couldn't afford to buy them all, so I read them in the store. . . . I found something that I liked in almost every book I read—cherry picking tips, advice, and practices and then applying them to my own process."[28]

Screenwriter Nathan Graham Davis learned a lot from online tutorials and social media groups. He says, "I did a 15-week course on YouTube designed to get you to the first draft of a script. It was done as a live class. . . . Those videos are still up [in 2024] and will still get you to a finished script in that amount of time, while also helping you build a good foundation for your craft."[29]

Skills and Personality

Almost every successful scriptwriter says the same thing: experience counts. Production studios rarely take a chance on a scriptwriter who does not have show business credentials. As screenwriting career coach Lee Jessup writes, "There is no screenwriting or TV writing career to be built without first mastering the craft. While writers in earlier stages of their careers have told me things like 'I know I could write better than that'. . . the craft question is not a hypothetical one; you prove your knowledge of and prowess with the craft on the page."[30]

A thick skin is necessary for a scriptwriter because rejection is part of the job. Around fifty thousand scripts are registered every year with the Writers Guild, the screenwriter's union. Only around 150 scripts get selected for production. And even scriptwriters who sell their work must deal with comments and suggestions from producers and directors. This can be extremely difficult for many writers. Scriptwriters need to be patient and willing to compromise when asked to do multiple rewrites. Persistence is also important. Scriptwriters who succeed have spent years cultivating relationships with Hollywood insiders, including agents, producers, directors, and actors.

Working Conditions

Scriptwriters are most often self-employed. They work at home or wherever they can find the best conditions for writing. Ron Osborn sets his alarm for 3:40 a.m. He says he can get more work done when the world is quiet and his phone is not buzzing. Scriptwriters also attend movie premiers, awards shows, and charity events where they might be able to meet producers and directors and pitch their ideas.

Employers and Earnings

Most scriptwriters create scripts on spec, short for *speculation*. Entertainment journalist Britton Perelman explains, "Writing something 'on spec' in Hollywood is just code for 'free.' No one is paying the writer to work on the script, nor is there any guarantee that the script will get made [into a film]."[31] A spec script might be presented to a talent manager or agent, who will try to sell it to a major movie studio like Sony or Paramount or to a specialty cable TV channel, such as Hallmark or MTV.

However, studios rarely buy scripts from unknown writers. Some scriptwriters build up their résumés by writing podcasts, videos, and commercials. Others begin their careers in entry-level entertainment industry jobs. They work as low-paid background actors or even security guards, just to gain access to studios. A scriptwriter known as "epizelus" worked as a production assistant, delivering coffee and running errands for producers, before being promoted to work as a writer's assistant, "All this time I was writing my own material and making sure my employers knew I was writing and wanted to be a screenwriter," epizelus states. "[I]

> ### Find a Buyer for Your Script
>
> "Find movies like your script and see which production companies made them. You can also watch similar movies and pay close attention to the few production companies and distributor logos that open the film. . . . You can also search for the writers of those movies and see who represents those types of writers. Once you have this information, try to find contact email addresses for as many relevant people as possible. This will be hit or miss, but email queries are the easiest ways to connect with companies. . . . Some may have policies against reading unsolicited material or emails . . . but that's part of the game."
>
> —Ken Miyamoto, screenwriter
>
> Ken Miyamoto, "10 Things I Did to Become a Professional Screenwriter," ScreenCraft, October 12, 2022. www.screencraft.org.

had a sample ready that fit the tone of our hit show."[32] In time, epizelus was hired as one of the writers on the show.

Those who dream of a career as a scriptwriter might imagine themselves in a writer's room on a TV series or earning millions of dollars as a big-time Hollywood writer. While some scriptwriters do achieve such success, Ken Miyamoto calls them the one per-centers, or the one out of a hundred who make it to the top. Most scriptwriters work odd jobs or at other careers while trying to sell their work. With all these factors taken into account, a scriptwriter can earn anywhere from $38,000 to $100,006 per year, according to the employment website Zippia. Those at the top of their game can earn millions.

Future Outlook

The Bureau of Labor Statistics does not compile statistics on script-writers but predicts that employment for all writers will increase by

4 percent through 2032. And the scriptwriting website ScreenCraft is optimistic about the job outlook for screenwriters. The growth in animation and streaming services means that there will be a bigger demand for screenwriters in the coming years.

Find Out More

American Screenwriters Association (ASA)
http://americanscreenwriters.com
The mission of the ASA is to help screenwriters develop their skills and sell their scripts. The ASA website features screenwriting tips, services, a free e-book, and news about the industry.

Sundance Institute
www.sundance.org
The Artist Programs offered by the Sundance Institute provide tools and training for young, independent storytellers. The institute's website offers information about labs, grants, and fellowships.

Writers Guild Foundation
www.wgfoundation.org
The Writers Guild Foundation has a huge library of free movie and television scripts online in multiple historic eras and genres. The Resource Center on the website also features links to scriptwriting classes, creative organizations, and primers on TV and movie screenwriting fundamentals.

Technical Writer

What Does a Technical Writer Do?

Almost everyone is familiar with the little printed booklets that are included with new products. The assembly instructions and how-to guides, which are also available online, are the work of technical writers. These professionals use their writing skills to simplify complex concepts for consumers, scientists, software coders, health care professionals, and others. Technical writer Dipo Ajose-Coker says people at parties often ask him to explain his job, so he uses his skills to describe his complex job in simple terms. He says:

> A technical writer is someone who helps people to understand how to use things like computers, mobile phones, machines, toys, and even medication. After the writer talks to the engineers who built or created the thing they need to write about, a technical writer then imagines they are the person that has to use the machine and finds a way to explain how to use, repair or maintain it in a way that is easy for them to understand.[33]

A Few Facts

Typical Earnings
$80,050 in 2023

Educational Requirements
Bachelor's degree in communications or a specialty field like engineering or computer information technology

Personal Qualities
Excellent communications skills, critical-thinking skills, attention to detail, time-management skills

Work Settings
Full time in offices, technology workrooms, and scientific laboratories

Future Outlook
Growth of 7 percent through 2032

Technical writers can be specialists who focus on a single product, procedure, or service. Some focus on computer applications and digital technology, writing customer support documents like user manuals and software tutorials. This job involves more than writing, as a technical writer named Jacklyn explains. "Any tech writer would be able to tell you that our job includes a lot more than just documentation. . . . Many of us have to understand programming or code at the same level as software developers."[34] In addition, technical writers often work with graphic artists and photographers to incorporate illustrations, charts, graphs, animation, videos, and photos into their work. Therefore, they must understand how words and images function together for explaining topics to an audience.

The words of technical writers are found on product websites, frequently-asked-question pages, help files, and social media sites. Those who specialize in business and finance write contracts, business proposals, and reports called white papers that cover complicated issues. Technical writers working in medicine and science write about clinical trials, laboratory equipment, and scientific reports for publication. Some technical writers are education specialists who create curricula, study guides, and workbooks. Those who focus on government agencies explain new laws and regulations in a user-friendly manner that makes policies more accessible to businesses and the public. Other technical writing categories include military hardware, automobiles and equipment, and engineering fields, including robotics, aeronautics, and electronics. Whatever their focus, technical writers need to have comprehensive knowledge of the field to provide error-free, high-quality instructions and information.

A Typical Workday

Like most workers, technical writers spend their initial work hours going through important emails and texts so they can prioritize

Working with Subject Matter Experts

"My job is at least 50-50 writing and meeting with people. SMEs [subject matter experts], managers, coworkers, project managers, editors—the list goes on. [Subject matter expert] interactions vary depending on the person. Very few people are easy to work with right from the start. SMEs tend to want us to write exactly what they want, how they want. . . . Nothing goes live without SME approval. We're not in charge of the processes, so if we have a question for the SME, we have to wait for them to answer. We can't just assume we know what needs to be on the page."

—Nofoofro, Reddit handle of a technical writer

Quoted in Reddit, "Day in the Life of a Technical Writer?," 2022. www.reddit.com.

their tasks for the day. They can expect to spend a good portion of their day on Slack, Zoom, and X (formerly Twitter). Technical writing involves teamwork, and workdays are often filled with meetings. Depending on the product, technical writers will meet with engineers, scientists, support specialists, salespeople, and corporate executives. Technical writers also work closely with professionals known as subject matter experts, who have advanced knowledge of a specific sector, practice, process, or piece of equipment.

A technical writer might follow the full development of a product from the planning stages through testing, production, and marketing. After a product is sold, technical writers remain engaged. They follow consumer comments and complaints and work with clients to improve usability.

Technical writers often juggle several projects that involve reading technical journals, conducting online research, and attending product design demos. This leaves only a few hours a day to sit down and write. Ajose-Coker calls these periods "writing sprints," and he sets his phone to "Do not disturb" when he

Empowering People with Technical Writing

"At my work, I actively encourage people from all parts of the business to contribute to our content, whether their contributions are technical writing, product explainers, or anything else that would help a customer or a member of our audience. I help brainstorm ideas, provide feedback, edit content, and more. . . . As a technical writer, you are tasked with knowing something inside out and distilling that knowledge into material that will help someone learn something new, create something, or solve a problem. With every paragraph, code snippet, and example, you can help someone feel more comfortable with a topic. You can educate, empower."

—JamesG, technical writer

JamesG, "My Experience Starting as a Technical Writer," *James' Coffee Blog*, November 27, 2023. https://jamesg.blog.

begins a sprint. "Setting aside writing sprint periods is one way to keep motivated, and maintaining focus as a technical writer," he says. "During a writing sprint, a technical writer sets aside a specific period of time, usually an hour or two, to focus solely on writing without any distractions."[35]

Technical writers who work as freelancers have additional tasks. They need to create and maintain portfolios of their work that feature writing samples that can be shown to prospective clients. Freelancers often join professional associations and attend conferences, where they can meet other technical writers and make network connections that might lead to writing opportunities.

Education and Training

Technical writers usually have a bachelor's degree in communications. Courses focus on nonfiction writing, business writing, marketing, and editing. A specialist might have a degree in engineering, computer science, or other related fields.

Some technical writers pick up their skills on the job. They train with other technical writers while learning how to write descriptively, rather than in the narrative style of a creative writer.

Technical writers may improve their opportunities for career advancement by pursuing certification through trade organizations. The Society for Technical Communication offers multitiered certification programs for entry-level writers, mid-level practitioners, and senior-level experts. Candidates who seek the Foundation Level Certification should have at least two years of professional study or work experience. Those on the senior level are expected to have five to ten years of experience. Similarly, certification from the American Medical Writers Association proves that a writer can create medical documents. This certification requires candidates to have a bachelor's degree and two years of experience in medical communications.

As with workers in other technology fields, technical writers need to self-educate throughout their careers. They must stay up-to-date on the latest industry trends and read trade journals, articles, and research papers that cover advancements in their sector.

Skills and Personality

The main job of a technical writer is to simplify complicated concepts using short sentences and basic language. Technical writers need good communications skills to create outlines and glossaries and write, proofread, and edit content. Writers also need to be able to communicate in plain language with clients and others who lack technical knowledge.

Critical-thinking skills and attention to detail are extremely important for technical writers; their information needs to be accurate and precise. Technical writers must be excellent researchers who can study complex subjects and interpret their findings. And technical writers need good time-management skills since they often work on several projects at the same time.

Working Conditions

Some technical writers work in offices forty hours a week or more when projects are nearing deadlines. They often sit at their desks in front of computers for long periods when working. Some are self-employed and work on short-term or recurring assignments in their home offices or elsewhere.

California-based technical writer Phil Davis works odd hours since his company has offices all over the world and he is the only one responsible for overseeing the company's documents. "Anything and everything related to documentation, I'm the ONLY guy. I start early (5am) to catch our offices in NYC and London and the tail end of [the workday in] Bangalore [India]. . . . Because of my early start, I'm usually able to knock off around 2pm to beat the traffic. Luckily, evening work and meetings are rare for me, so I can get some time with the family and [to] be rested and ready for the next day."[36]

Employers and Earnings

Technical writers often become proficient by first working as technical specialists or research assistants. After developing an extensive knowledge of their discipline, they might take communications courses or train with experienced writers within a company to assume technical writing tasks.

Employers of technical writers include product manufacturers, scientific and technical companies, professional services, publishers, and government agencies. A technical writer who blogs under the name JamesG offers this tip to prospective writers:

> I have found technology startups to be an excellent place to look for technical writing roles. These roles often pair with other responsibilities and fall under a marketing team. . . . I don't know a lot about larger companies, but I do know that there is always a need for someone who can document software. From the smallest Python package to the largest database solution in the world, documentation is essential.[37]

The Bureau of Labor Statistics (BLS) says the median annual income for technical writers in 2023 was $80,050. Those in the lowest-paid 10 percent made less than $48,630, while the top-earning technical writers averaged $129,440.

Future Outlook

The BLS says the technical writing profession will grow by 7 percent through 2032, faster than the average for all occupations. This translates to around forty-eight hundred job openings for technical writers annually. As scientific and technological knowledge continues to grow along with consumer demand for new products, technical writers will be needed to convert complex information into user-friendly copy.

Find Out More

American Medical Writers Association (AMWA)
www.amwa.org
The AMWA is an educational and resource center for writers who specialize in medical communications. Its website offers career advancement information, including webinars, tips for freelancers, editing guides, and several certification programs.

National Association of Science Writers (NASW)
www.nasw.org
Journalists, authors, and editors who belong to the National Association of Science Writers can receive various awards, grants, and fellowships and can network at the annual Science Writers convention. The NASW website offers handbooks and field guides with information for students and freelancers.

Society for Technical Communication (STC)
www.stc.org
The STC is a professional organization of technical writers. Its website hosts a job bank, academic databases, educational webinars, student scholarships, online seminars, blogs, and certification programs.

Grant Writer

What Does a Grant Writer Do?

Most businesses exist to make a profit. But according to the National Center for Charitable Statistics, there are more than 1.5 million institutions in the United States known as nonprofit organizations, or NPOs. These organizations have a mission to improve people's lives and benefit society rather than earn a profit. Nonprofit organizations include a wide range of public charities, private foundations, community clinics, museums, educational institutions, youth groups, environmental groups, scientific and research associations, and religious organizations.

Nonprofit organizations depend on donations called grants. Grants are sums of money—ranging from hundreds to millions of dollars—that are donated by individuals, corporations, foundations, and government agencies. And grant writers are an important link between NPOs and donors. Grant writers secure funding for their organizations by writing detailed grant proposals and submitting them to agencies that provide funding.

Writing successful grant proposals requires a great deal of research. Grant writers need to find donors that have the same goals as their organization. This requires grant writers to

A Few Facts

Typical Earnings
$75,477 in 2024

Educational Requirements
Bachelor's degree in English, communications, journalism, marketing, or business

Personal Qualities
Good communication skills, good researcher, organized, self-starter, team player

Work Settings
40 hours a week or more in offices

Future Outlook
Growth of 6 percent through 2028

search through dozens of donor websites, funder lists, and other databases on the internet. Research provides information about a funder's mission, past projects, and the types of grants given out. And every donor group has specific guidelines for awarding grants, some of which can be quite complex. Grant writers need to thoroughly understand a donor's eligibility requirements before taking the next step in the process: writing a grant proposal, which consists of several documents.

The main task of the grant writer is to demonstrate an organization's commitment to the donor's mission and to prove that the NPO has the background and experience to use the funds wisely. A proposal begins with an introduction that outlines the project that needs funding, including what it will cost and how long it will take. Grant writers need to clearly describe the positive impact the project will have on individuals and the community. This requires the writer to tell a compelling story that grabs the donor's attention. According to grant writing educator Meredith Noble, "Your constituents and community are the driving force behind your entire mission and all your work. Make sure this is abundantly clear in your grant proposal by anchoring your stories and details with real people. Specificity and authenticity are much more appealing to readers than vague hypotheticals."[38]

In addition to the proposal, grant writers need to create a good cover letter and a detailed budget that includes the NPO's tax and financial statements. A grant writer usually illustrates points with photographs, charts, graphs, and statistics. The writer must provide supporting documents, including a detailed list of the past and present activities of the NPO. Letters of support, good reviews, and recommendations from community members who have benefited from the work of the NPO are also required.

Make a Compelling Case

"The entire [grant] application should tell a story. A story does not need characters. Instead, it has a logical flow that moves the reader from one idea to the next. Your application should seamlessly move from the needs statement to your project plan and into your evaluation and budget, leaving no 'plot holes' or unresolved issues, just like a good Jane Austen novel. Re-read your application to see if you tell a good story. If not, edit until you do, getting rid of all the extraneous details that do not belong in this story."

—M. Linda Wastyn, fundraising executive

M. Linda Wastyn, "Tell Stories to Make Your Case for Funding More Compelling," Grant Professionals Association, August 10, 2021. www.grantprofessionals.org.

A Typical Workday

Grant writers spend a good portion of the day responding to emails, texts, and phone calls with donors and potential donors while searching for new funding opportunities. If a grant writer finds a funding organization that might be a good fit, he or she often reads through successful proposals from the past. These old documents, which are usually a matter of public record, help a grant writer get an idea of what to include in a new proposal and how best to appeal to the donor. Once a grant proposal is completed, grant writers carefully proofread their work and double check facts and figures. Grant proposals might be rejected for even small mistakes.

Grant writers often prioritize their work using detailed calendars that help them keep track of client meetings, grant proposal deadlines, and upcoming events. A grant writer with the handle LMP34 says a good calendar is important because "[you] need to be the kind of person who can plan ahead and not leave things

Although grant writers often work in home offices, they have frequent meetings with the groups they work with. Collaboration enables grant writers to create strong proposals on the group's behalf.

to the last minute."[39] Planning ahead is necessary because NPOs might be staffed by volunteers who are slow to respond to document requests. With deadlines looming, grant writers have to build their schedules to anticipate such delays.

A grant writer known as 2001Steel finds artificial intelligence helpful for scheduling: "I use ChatGPT to help me craft a fairly detailed workplan for myself. With the right inputs it can help with short, medium and long term goals. Just tell it a little about yourself, the [organization]—how it's structured, its programs . . . and then ask it to develop a plan. Pretty solid output that you can tweak."[40]

Education and Training

Grant writers often have a bachelor's degree in English, journalism, creative writing, communications, marketing, or business.

Those who wish to work with large donors and international organizations might need a master's degree.

Prospective grant writers can gain experience in high school by volunteering at a local nonprofit such as an environmental organization, community food bank, arts council, or animal welfare group. Many of these organizations have intern programs in which students can learn by working with grant writers and other personnel.

Certification will help anyone interested in pursuing a career in grant writing. The programs offered by the American Grant Writers' Association (AGWA) are similar to those offered by colleges and other professional organizations. The AGWA Certified Grant Writer Series is aimed at students. Candidates take online courses that focus on research methods, grant opportunities, statistics gathering, and writing proposals and other materials. When courses are completed, students receive accreditation after passing an online exam.

Skills and Personality

Grant writers use their skills to produce a very specific type of document, but the rules of good writing apply to anyone who excels in this field. As best-selling writer Stephen King notes, "If you want to be a writer, you must do two things above all others: read a lot and write a lot. There's no way around these two things that I'm aware of, no shortcut."[41] While grant writers do not produce thrilling horror stories like King, this is great advice. Grant writer Amanda Day explains:

> As grant professionals, we write. We tell stories. We share information. Through the written word we convince readers to award our organization funding to implement the thoughtful plan we have so perfectly described in 500

words or less. So, why is reading so vital to your development as a grant writer? It fires up your brain! When you read more than bland grant instructions, you learn new words. You understand the power of sentence structure. You see how the use of white space can impact the ease of reading. You feel the cadence of a paragraph. You see what works."[42]

While writing can be fun, grant writing is highly competitive. Donors receive numerous funding requests, and there is no guarantee that a proposal will be successful. This can make grant writing stressful. Writers need to keep cool under pressure and while working long hours to meet deadlines. That is why LMP34 says, "You need to be organized, have a lot of self-discipline, be a self-starter, and enjoy working by yourself."[43]

Working Conditions

Grant writers who are employed by NPOs usually work in offices, although some might work remotely. Self-employed grant writers generally work in home offices. Wherever they conduct business, grant writers often work nights and weekends. They look for funding opportunities outside regular work hours and often have to quickly write up complex proposals.

Grant writing can be a demanding activity, and some say the work can be boring. However, an unnamed grant writer on the Ascend NBS website has a different take: "A constant in the life of a grant writer is meeting and collaborating with interesting people who are committed to improving the world. A sense of satisfaction is felt in the heart of the grant writer when an important mission is rewarded with financial support. Think of the positive feelings you'd get if you secured funding for an important initiative!"[44]

Gather as Much Information as Possible

"My days are filled with emails and/or meetings to move projects forward so they're closer to being grant ready, chipping away at multiple applications or reports, researching funding opportunities for clients, and networking/setting up meetings for clients with potential partners, funders, and/or elected officials. When I start relationships with new clients, I always ask them to give me access to any and everything they think might help me write. This can include old grant applications, both successful and unsuccessful (I find both helpful), previous financial documents, budgets, one-pagers, press releases, etc. I've always found that having more than I need is better than constantly asking for documents."

—philanthropy_watch, Reddit name of a manager of a US grant writing firm

philanthropy_watch, "Any Grant Writers Here?," Reddit, 2023. www.reddit.com.

Employers and Earnings

Grant writers are often freelancers, but some work full time in the nonprofit sector, which can include government organizations, community clinics, museums, educational institutions, youth groups, environmental groups, and scientific and research associations. Some of the biggest NPOs in the United States include United Way Worldwide, American National Red Cross, and Feeding America. Other well-known NPOs include the YMCA, Goodwill Industries, and the Boys & Girls Clubs of America. There are countless smaller NPOs that also rely on the work of professional grant writers.

In 2024 the average annual salary for a grant writer was $75,477, according to the website Salary.com. The highest earners were making around $93,474, while the grant writers with the lowest salaries earned $60,757 annually.

Future Outlook

The Bureau of Labor Statistics (BLS) does not have a separate category for grant writers. The BLS says the job outlook for all writers is expected to shrink by 4 percent through 2032. However, with more than 1 million NPOs relying on grant writers to bring in funding, the outlook for grant writers is brighter. According to the career website Zippia, the projected growth for grant writers is 6 percent through 2028.

Find Out More

American Grant Writers' Association (AGWA)
www.agwa.us

The AGWA provides online courses, grant writing services, and certification. Its website offers information about grant writing standards and ethics and a grant writing FAQ section.

Association of Fundraising Professionals (AFP)
https://afpglobal.org

The AFP has been offering training, support, and career advice to grant writers for more than sixty years. Students can find grant writing guidelines and a donor bill of rights on the AFP website.

Grant Professionals Association (GPA)
https://grantprofessionals.org

The GPA has extensive educational offerings, with webinars, blogs, and career development and employment information. Grant writers can sign up for career coaching sessions and help with résumé writing.

Source Notes

Introduction: For the Love of Words
1. Julia Angwin, "Press Pause on the Silicon Valley Hype Machine," *New York Times*, May 15, 2024. www.nytimes.com.
2. John Lopez, "AI May Kill Us All, but It'll Never Write a Good Movie," *Vanity Fair*, July 11, 2023. www.vanityfair.com.
3. Zawn Villines, "Advice for Making a Career as a Writer, and How I Became a Writer," Liberating Motherhood, August 26, 2023. https://zawn.substack.com.
4. Lopez, "AI May Kill Us All, but It'll Never Write a Good Movie."

Content Marketing Manager
5. Hayley Folk, "How to Run a Marketing Team with Hive," Hive, April 7, 2022. https://hive.com.
6. Gabriel Lumagui, "Artificial Intelligence and the Future of Content Marketing," *Forbes*, December 22, 2023. www.forbes.com.
7. Alexa Collins, "Marketing Funnels Explained: Why It Matters and How to Build Yours," Shopify, August 16, 2023. www.shopify.com.
8. Quoted in Kaya Ismail, "How to Optimize Bottom of the Funnel Content," CMSWire, May 20, 2020. www.cmswire.com.
9. Quoted in Reddit, "How Does a Day in the Life of a Content Marketer/Manager Look Like?," 2021. www.reddit.com.
10. Justin Paulsen, "How to Become a Content Marketing Manager," Tech Guide, May 13, 2024. https://techguide.org.

Public Relations Specialist
11. Quoted in Phil Hood, "Promoting Your Band: A Conversation with PR Maven Amanda Cagan," *Drum!*, 2024. https://drummagazine.com.
12. Quoted in Reddit, "What Is It like Working in a Public Relations Agency?," 2021. www.reddit.com.
13. Quoted in Carol Ann Underwood, "The Life of a Publicist," Plank Center, 2021. https://plankcenter.ua.edu.

14. Quoted in Underwood, "The Life of a Publicist."
15. Quoted in Bold Journey, "Meet Amanda Cagan," February 20, 2024. https://boldjourney.com.
16. Quoted in Reddit, "What Is It like Working in a Public Relations Agency?"
17. Quoted in Reddit, "What Is It like Working in a Public Relations Agency?"

Editor

18. Stephen King, *On Writing.* New York: Scribner, 2000, p. 10.
19. Megan Close Zavala, "A Day in the Life of a Book Editor," LinkedIn, October 5, 2022. www.linkedin.com.
20. Quoted in Vault Careers, "A Day in the Life: Book Editor," Vault, May 1, 2021. https://vault.com.
21. Tonya Thompson, "A Day in the Life of a Freelance Writer," Servicescape, December 27, 2019. www.servicescape.com.
22. Quoted in Phon Baillie, "A Day in the Life of a Work-at-Home Proofreader and Editor," Edit Republic, 2024. https://editrepublic.com.
23. Thompson, "A Day in the Life of a Freelance Writer."
24. Stephanie Leguichard, "How to Make $30/Hr Freelance Editing (Without Having to Find Clients)," Writing Cooperative, August 31, 2020. https://writingcooperative.com.

Scriptwriter

25. Geoffrey D. Calhoun, "What Does a Screenwriter Actually Do?," Successful Screenwriter, May 21, 2024. https://thesuccessfulscreenwriter.com.
26. Quoted in Ron Peterson and Cheryl G. Agbunag, "A Day in the Life of a Screenwriter," Film Connection, September 10, 2019. www.filmconnection.com.
27. Luke Leighfield, "How to Write a Script (Step-by-Step Guide)," Boords, March 3, 2024. https://boords.com.
28. Ken Miyamoto, "10 Things I Did to Become a Professional Screenwriter," ScreenCraft, October 12, 2022. https://screencraft.org.
29. Quoted in KillerMoth09, "How Did You Guys Succeed with Screenwriting?," Reddit, 2024. www.reddit.com.

30. Lee Jessup, "Screenwriting," Lee Jessup Career Coaching, January 4, 2021. https://leejessup.com.
31. Britton Perelman, "What Is a Spec Script (and Why Should You Write One)?," ScreenCraft, May 9, 2023. https://screencraft.org.
32. Quoted in KillerMoth09, "How Did You Guys Succeed with Screenwriting?"

Technical Writer

33. Dipo Ajose-Coker, "Day in the Life: Story of a Tech Writer," Componize, January 24, 2024. https://componize.com.
34. Jacklyn, "A Typical Day for a Technical Writer," Medium, March 2, 2019. https://medium.com.
35. Ajose-Coker, "A Day in the Life."
36. Quoted in Jacklyn, "A Typical Day for a Technical Writer."
37. JamesG, "My Experience Starting as a Technical Writer," *James' Coffee Blog*, November 27, 2023. https://jamesg.blog.

Grant Writer

38. Meredith Noble, "Storytelling for Grant Writers: 10 Tactical & Stylistic Tips," Achieve Causes, March 18, 2024. www.achievecauses.com.
39. LMP34, "What Does a Day in the Life of a Nonprofit Grant-Writer Look Like?," Reddit, 2023. www.reddit.com.
40. 2001Steel, "Any Grant Writers Here?," Reddit, 2023. www.reddit.com.
41. King, *On Writing*, p. 10.
42. Amanda Day, "Readers Make Better Grant Writers," Grant Professionals Association, December 12, 2023. https://grantprofessionals.org.
43. LMP34, "What Does a Day in the Life of a Nonprofit Grant-Writer Look Like?"
44. Ascend NBS, "Is Grant Writing a Good Career?," April 23, 2024. https://ascendnbs.com.

Interview with a Grant Writer

Ashley Pereira began her career as a grant writer in 2008 and now runs her own firm, Greater Good Consultants. She conducted this interview with the author by email.

Q: Why did you become a grant writer?
A: I started out as a middle and high school science teacher. Working in the inner city, I often had to write grants to fund my classroom projects. I became a grant writer because I loved the nature of the job. It is exciting to search for funding, craft a data-driven story, and win!

Q: Can you describe your typical workday?
A: As an entrepreneur I am blessed to be able to create my own schedule. I start work early in the morning by checking and responding to emails. Then I check my grant databases to see if there are any new opportunities or projects. I spend the rest of my day meeting with clients online and working on grant research, grant writing, and strategy development.

Q: What do you like most about your job?
A: My favorite part of this job is that it is like a treasure hunt! It is also very rewarding to help people doing important work get the funding they need to help even more people.

Q: What do you like least about your job?
A: The worst part of this career is the tight deadlines that are often associated with grants. Sometimes I have to work long hours before a deadline, and it can be stressful. For example, once I was hired to complete a 12-page grant proposal for a new client that

was due in 24 hours. Since it was a new client, I had to start from scratch, which takes an incredible amount of time. I had to stay up late (nearly to midnight), then woke up around 5 am to resume writing in order to finish the job on time. If you miss a deadline most funders will not even consider your application. I am proud to say that I have never missed a deadline. But I have missed out on sleep from time to time!

Q: What personal qualities do you find most valuable for this type of work?
A: The most important quality is to care about something specific. For example, I am very passionate about education and only work for education-related organizations. My passion to make a difference in this field is what fuels my success. The second most important quality to me is organization. You must be highly organized and self-motivated to successfully manage the many pieces involved in grants.

Q: What advice do you have for students who might be interested in this career?
A: My advice is to get started in the field as soon as you can. While I was still in high school, I started volunteering for a family friend to assist with grant-related tasks. This helped me see what the career entailed, and [the volunteer work] was very impressive on my résumé as I advanced in my career. You need to try it to see if you like it, so get started now!

Q: What types of projects are you currently working on?
A: Right now, I am working on many different types of projects with many types of clients, which is something I really love about my job. I enjoy variety, and each day is unique! One project is serving as a Technical Assistance provider for a federal grant program in Oregon. In this role I meet with potential applicants and

help them in the application process. This is a great program, as I am able to build the capacity of small nonprofits and help them apply to a grant that may otherwise be impossible.

Another project I am working on right now is for an immersive technology company. I am helping them to find grants that match and prepare templates that they can use in future grant applications. This not only helps them, but also makes it easy for educators to get the tools and technologies they need to truly engage students in STEM. As a former science teacher, it is very gratifying to be able to still help students even though I am no longer teaching in the classroom.

Other Jobs If You Like Writing

Announcer
Blogger
Business-to-business writer
Communications planner
Copywriter
Digital media supervisor
Email marketer
English teacher
Ghostwriter
Literary agent
Multimedia communications specialist
News analyst
Novelist
Online communications director
Online content coordinator
Podcaster
Poet
Reporter
Science writer
Search engine optimization content writer
Social media manager
Social media relations director
Songwriter
Video game writer
Web developer

Editor's note: The online *Occupational Outlook Handbook* of the US Department of Labor's Bureau of Labor Statistics is an excellent source of information on jobs in hundreds of career fields, including many of those listed here. The *Occupational Outlook Handbook* may be accessed online at www.bls.gov/ooh.

Index

Note: Boldface page numbers indicate illustrations.

acquisition editors, 24
Ajose-Coker, Dipo, 39, 41–42
American Association of Advertising Agencies (4A's), 14
American Copy Editors Society (ACES), 26–27, 29
American Grant Writers' Association (AGWA), 51, 54
American Marketing Association (AMA), 14
American Medical Writers Association (AMWA), 43, 45
American Screenwriters Association (ASA), 38
American Society of Magazine Editors (ASME), 30
artificial intelligence (AI), 5
　in content marketing, 8
Association of Fundraising Professionals (AFP), 54

Baillie, Phon, 28
Bureau of Labor Statistics (BLS), 61
　on content marketing manager, 12, 13–14
　on editor, 27–29
　on job outlook for writers/authors, 6
　on public relations specialist, 21
　on technical writer, 45
　on writer, 6, 37–38, 54
business-to-business (B2B) communications, 5

Cagan, Amanda, 15–16, 17, 18–19
Calhoun, Geoffrey D., 31
Content Marketing Institute, 14
content marketing manager, **10**
　education/training requirements, 7, 11
　employers of, 12
　future job outlook, 7, 13–14
　information on, 14
　role of, 7–8
　salary/earnings, 7, 12
　skills/personal qualities, 7, 11–12
　typical workday, 8–11
　working conditions, 12
　work settings, 7
copy editor, 23–24
Cricket (magazine), 4

Davis, Nathan Graham, 35
Davis, Phil, 44
Davis, Russell, 24–25
developmental editor, 23–24

editor
  education/training requirements, 23, 26–27
  employers of, 27–28
  future job outlook, 23, 28–29
  information on, 29–30
  role of, 23–24
  salary/earnings, 23, 28
  skills/personal qualities, 23, 27
  typical workday, 24–26
  working conditions, 27
  work settings, 23
executive editors, 24

Folk, Hayley, 7

Gaskin, Deidre, 17, 18
Grant Professionals Association (GPA), 54
grant writer, **50**
  education/training requirements, 47, 50–51
  employers of, 53
  future job outlook, 47, 54
  information on, 54
  interview with, 58–60
  role of, 47–48
  salary/earnings, 47, 53
  skills/personal qualities, 47, 51–52
  typical workday, 49–50
  working conditions, 52
  work settings, 47

Hogan, Breanna, 20
Hootsuite Academy, 22

International Association of Business Communicators (IABC), 22

Jessup, Lee, 35

King, Stephen, 23, 51

Leguichard, Stephanie, 29
Leighfield, Luke, 32–33
Literary Orphans (magazine), 4
loglines, 32
Lopez, John, 5, 6
Lumagui, Gabriel, 8

Micallef, Annette, 13
Mitchell, Heather, 27
Miyamoto, Ken, 34–35, 37

National Association of Science Writers (NASW), 46
National Center for Charitable Statistics, 47
Noble, Meredith, 48
nonprofit organizations (NPOs), 47

Occupational Outlook Handbook (Bureau of Labor Statistics), 61
Osborn, Ron, 32, 36

Paulsen, Justin, 12
Pereira, Ashley, 58–60
press secretary, 16
public relations specialist, **19**

education/training
   requirements, 15, 17–18
employers of, 21
future job outlook, 15, 21
information on, 22
role of, 15–16
salary/earnings, 15, 21
skills/personal qualities, 15,
   18–20
typical workday, 16–17
working conditions, 21
work settings, 15
Public Relations Student Society
   of America (PRSSA), 22

sales/marketing funnel, 9–10
Saul, Ryan, 33
Scribbr (website), 26, 30
Scribendi (website), 26
scriptwriter, **34**
   education/training
     requirements, 31, 34–35
   employers of, 36–37
   future job outlook, 31, 37–38
   information on, 38
   role of, 31–32
   salary/earnings, 31, 37
   skills/personal qualities, 31,
     35–36
   typical workday, 32–33
   working conditions, 36
   work settings, 31
Search Engine Journal, 8
search engine optimization
   (SEO), 7–8

Smolan, Lindsey, 16
Society for Technical
   Communication (STC), 43,
   46
Storrs, Marissa, 9
Sundance Institute, 38

technical writer
   education/training
     requirements, 39, 42–43
   employers of, 44–45
   future job outlook, 39, 45
   information on, 45–46
   role of, 39–40
   salary/earnings, 39, 45
   skills/personal qualities, 39,
     43–44
   typical workday, 40–42
   working conditions, 44
   work settings, 39
Thompson, Tonya, 25–26,
   29

Villines, Zawn, 6

Wastyn, M. Linda, 49
Writers Guild Foundation, 38
writers/writing
   Bureau of Labor Statistics
     on, 6, 37–38, 54
   other jobs in, 61
   See also grant writer;
     scriptwriter; technical writer

Zavala, Megan Close, 24